LEGENDS OF WARFARE

GROUND

M40 Gun Motor Carriage

and M43 Howitzer Motor Carriage in WWII and Korea

DAVID DOYLE

Schiffer Publishing Ltd

4880 Lower Valley Road • Atglen, PA 19310

Designed by Justin Watkinson
Type set in Impact/Minion Pro/Univers LT Std

All photos are from the collections of the US National Archives and Records Administration unless otherwise noted.

ISBN: 978-0-7643-5402-1
Printed in China

Published by Schiffer Publishing, Ltd.
4880 Lower Valley Road
Atglen, PA 19310
Phone: (610) 593-1777; Fax: (610) 593-2002
E-mail: Info@schifferbooks.com
www.schifferbooks.com

For our complete selection of fine books on this and related subjects, please visit our website at www.schifferbooks.com. You may also write for a free catalog.

Schiffer Publishing's titles are available at special discounts for bulk purchases for sales promotions or premiums. Special editions, including personalized covers, corporate imprints, and excerpts, can be created in large quantities for special needs. For more information, contact the publisher.

We are always looking for people to write books on new and related subjects. If you have an idea for a book, please contact us at proposals@schifferbooks.com.

Acknowledgments

This book would not have been possible without the gracious help of many individuals and institutions. Beyond the invaluable help provided by the staffs of the National Archives and the Patton Museum, as well as Gordon Blaker and the staff of the US Army Artillery Museum, I am indebted to Tom Kailbourn, Scott Taylor, Steve Zaloga, Dana Bell, John Blackman, Verne Kindschi, and Massimo Foti. Their generous and skillful assistance adds immensely to the quality of this volume. In addition to such wonderful friends and colleagues, the Lord has blessed me with a wonderful wife, Denise, who has tirelessly scanned thousands of photos and documents for this and numerous other books. Beyond that, she is an ongoing source of support and inspiration.

Contents

Introduction

When the United States initially became involved in World War II, the principal American 155 mm cannon was the French-designed, World War I-era M1917 Grande Puissance Filloux (GPF) like this example seen in Newfoundland, in May 1942. Although it had been superseded by the M1, production of the latter was slow to ramp up. *National Archives and Records Administration*

During the early years of World War II the US military was slow to embrace heavy self-propelled artillery. The initial production 155 mm Gun Motor Carriage fielded by the US military was the M12. Combining the French-designed M1917 Grande Puissance Filloux (GPF) gun with modified M3 medium tank chassis, one hundred of the M12 were produced between September 1942 and March 1943. The vehicles languished in storage for almost a year before finally being deployed. Once fielded, the M12 was recognized as a success, but the lack of additional M1917 guns and the growing obsolescence of the M3 chassis precluded further production.

While production of the French 155 mm GPF had been licensed by the US during World War I, and domestic production of the weapon as the M1918 initiated—some of which were later also used to arm the M12—work toward developing an improved, longer-range 155 soon began. The first of these efforts was the M1920, but work was curtailed due to post-World War I budget cuts. The 155 mm cannon was again addressed in 1929 with the T4, with the objective of increased range. With slight modifications, the T4 was standardized in 1938 as the 155 mm Gun M1. On June 12, 1941, after only twenty M1 guns had been produced, production shifted to the M1A1, which dispensed with the breech-ring bushing, instead cutting the breech threads directly into the breech ring.

Concurrently with the development of the T4 gun, development of the T2 carriage was underway. This carriage, which featured split trails, tandem axles, and dual pneumatic wheels, was standardized in 1938, becoming the ubiquitous M1 carriage.

The drawback of the M1/M1A1 was mobility, just as had been the case with the M1917/M1918. Given the hesitance to field self-propelled weapons, the 155s were first towed by slow speed tractors, such as the D7 Caterpillar, and later by the powerful Mack NO 7½-ton 6x6 truck, which in time was augmented by the fully-tracked M4 high-speed tractor. Regardless of prime mover, emplacing the weapon into a firing position was a laborious and time-consuming operation.

Emplacement time was an even greater concern with the 155's high-firing twin, the 8-in Howitzer M1, which required a pit be dug beneath the breech to allow firing at maximum elevation. Emplacement times were noted as being variable, from thirty minutes to six hours. Development of the 8-inch howitzer closely mimicked that of the 155 mm cannon. Into the 1930s, US forces were armed with British-designed 8-inch howitzers dating to World War I. A 1920s development program for an improved weapon, the M1920, languished due to budgetary issues. Revived in 1927 with a new forged barrel, the improved artillery piece was designated the 8-inch Howitzer T3. In time the T3 was standardized as the 8-inch Howitzer M1. While the carriage was the same as that used for the M1A1 155 mm gun, the recoil system configuration differed owing to the differences in recoil forces and tube weights between the weapons.

The US-designed M1 and M1A1 155 mm cannons were potent pieces of field artillery, however mobility was an issue. Mounted on the classic M1 carriage, the cannons were initially towed by slow speed tractors, like this example in Oran, Algeria, coupled to an International Harvester TD-18 in April 1943. Later, high-speed tractors and wheeled prime movers were utilized. *National Archives and Records Administration*

The first successful US vehicle mounting the 155 mm cannon was the M12 Gun Motor Carriage. Built around the automotive components of the M3 medium tank, and armed with the World War I vintage 155 mm Gun M1917, M1917A1, and M1918A1, Pressed Steel Car Company produced one hundred examples of the M12. *National Archives and Records Administration*

GENERAL DATA STANDARD NOMENCLATURE LIST G-232

MODEL	M40 (T83)	M43 (T89)
Combat weight, pounds*	81,000	80,000
Length, spade in traveling position**	357	289
Width**	124	124
Height**	129.75	129.75
Track	101	101
Std track width	23	23
Crew	8	8
Max speed, mph	24	24
Fuel capacity, gallons	215	215
Range, miles	107	107
Electrical	24 neg. ground	24 neg. ground
Transmission speeds	5	5
Turning radius feet	41.5	41.5
Armament	155 mm M1A1 or M2	8-inch M1 or M2
Mount	M13	M17
Traverse	36-degrees	36-degrees
Elevation	-5 to 45 degrees	-5 to 45 degrees
Maximum range, high explosive	25,715 yards	18,510 yards
Telescopes	M69F & M16A1F	M69G & M16A1G
Panoramic telescope	M12	
Gunners quadrant		M1
Ammunition stowage	20 rounds	16 rounds

*Weight with crew, fuel, and ammunition
**Overall dimensions listed in inches.

ENGINE DATA

Engine make/model*	Continental R975-C4
Number of cylinders	9 radial
Cubic inch displacement	973
Horsepower	400 @ 2400
Torque	940 @ 1700
Governed speed (rpm)	2400

RADIO EQUIPMENT

Provisions for an SCR-610 set with RC-99 interphone, or SCR-608B with integral interphone, or SCR-619 or British Wireless Set No.19 in sponson to the right of the assistant driver.

CHAPTER 1

Development of the T83

As production of the M12 was completed, on April 13, 1943, the chief of ordnance requested that a study be made concerning the development of a suitable gun motor carriage for the 155 mm Gun M1 and the 8-inch Howitzer M1. The initial study revealed that neither of these weapons could be mounted on the M12 chassis, as the resultant vehicle would have excessive height and weight, and very limited traverse, yielding poor automotive and combat performance. Further study led to the decision to pursue mounting the new weapons on a chassis adapted from the new T23 medium tank, with gas-electric drive. The 155 mm Gun Motor Carriage on this chassis was to be designated T79, while the 8-inch howitzer-armed version was the T80. However, objections to the T79 were raised by Army Ground Forces because as designed the mount did not allow depression of the gun below horizontal. Once the T23 project was terminated, the T79 too was abandoned.

Building on the foundation established with the M12, on March 9, 1944, the Ordnance Committee by OCM 23098, recommended development of "a medium weight, high speed, large caliber self-propelled gun, which can be used for direct and indirect fire in support of rapidly moving armored vehicles."

This recommendation was approved on March 23, 1944, and the Ordnance Department was authorized to procure five pilot vehicles of a new-design 155 mm Gun Motor Carriage. The new vehicle would be armed with the 155 mm M1A1 gun and would utilize the automotive components of the M4 medium tank, albeit on a widened chassis. The vehicle was to utilize the then-newly developed horizontal volute suspension system and twenty-three-inch wide track. Pressed Steel Car Company of Hegewisch (Chicago), Illinois was awarded the contract to design and produce the pilot models, which would be designated T83.

The agreed schedule was that Pressed Steel would assemble the first pilot during the week of June 26, 1944, with the remaining four pilots to be completed in September. In fact, the first pilot was completed on July 28, and after a demonstration at Hegewisch was shipped to Aberdeen Proving Ground for evaluation.

While at Aberdeen the T83 completed a 500-mile endurance test and 200 rounds of 155 mm ammunition were fired. After other tests, the initial pilot was returned to Pressed Steel for modification according to production drawings.

On October 15, the second pilot T83 was shipped to Ft. Bragg for evaluation by the Field Artillery Board, with the third pilot being shipped on October 23, to same destination. During the following month each vehicle was driven about 1,500 miles as well as being used to evaluate the service of the piece and crew drills. As a result of these tests the design of the vehicle was modified to reflect minor changes to stowage as well as provide more working space in the hull and increase the usable area of the rear platform.

Subsequent to these tests and resultant modification of pilots 2 and 3, representatives of Army Ground Forces, Army Service Forces, Aberdeen Proving Ground, Office of Chief of Ordnance Detroit, and Pressed Steel Car Company met on December 11–12, 1944, in order to finalize the design prior to initiating series production. Among the changes agreed to was the relocation of the platform winch from the right to the left side of the hull and increasing the size of the rear hull opening, with an equal enlargement of the folding platform.

Based on the success in combat of the 155 mm Gun Motor Carriage M12 (or 155 mm GMC M12), the US Army began development of a vehicle with a larger chassis and a more potent 155 mm gun. Pressed Steel Car Company of Chicago was again contracted for the new vehicle, which was designated the 155 mm Gun Motor Carriage T83. The T83 featured a chassis based on that of the Medium Tank M4 with E8 suspension (HVSS). The first 155 mm GMC T83, seen here, bore the nickname "BIG SHOT" in white letters on the side. *National Archives and Records Administration*

The first pilot 155 mm GMC T83 was completed on July 28, 1944, and in this photo, Army officers are receiving a briefing on this new vehicle at its official rollout at the Pressed Steel Car Company in Chicago. For the occasion, a US flag and the two-star flag of a major general are flying from the vehicle. The T83 was equipped with cast-steel T66 tracks that were twenty-three inches wide, with a pitch (front-to-rear measurement) of six inches. A spotlight was mounted on top of the right side of the gun shield. *Military History Institute*

The T83 had a rear-mounted spade to stabilize the vehicle during the firing of the 155 mm gun. A manual winch was mounted inside the right rear of the fighting compartment to operate a cable that raised and lowered the spade. This winch later would be moved to the left rear of the fighting compartment.
A tailgate with hinges on the bottom was mounted on the rear of the hull. The grille that is secured to the tailgate was a loading ramp, which was hinged to the top of the tailgate.
National Archives and Records Administration

The tailgate of the T83 is extended and the loading ramp is deployed, resting on a folding support, allowing a view inside the fighting compartment. The T83s were armed with the 155 mm Gun M1A1 or M2 on the 155 mm Gun Mount T14. On the left side of the gun carriage is the traversing hand wheel. Also visible are the breech block of the gun and the operating cable for the tailgate, which is routed through an opening on the right rear of the hull and around pulleys on the tailgate and the left side of the rear of the hull. *National Archives and Records Administration*

The first pilot 155 mm Gun Motor Carriage T83 is seen from the upper left rear with the tailgate and loading ramp extended. Cupolas with six direct-vision blocks were provided for the driver and the assistant driver. Unlike the gun mount of the 155 mm GMC M12, the T83's had equilibrator assemblies to each side of the gun. These units served to counterbalance the long gun, requiring less strenuous elevation of the gun at lower elevations. *National Archives and Records Administration*

The fighting compartment of the T83 had storage compartments on the right and left sides. The engine compartment was to the front of the fighting compartment, while the driver's and assistant driver's compartment was to the front of the engine compartment. Pioneer tools and several ventilation grilles were on the deck over the engine compartment. In the front right corner of the fighting compartment can be seen two horizontal tubes: these were the top tier of a five-tier projectile rack, with a similar rack on the opposite side of the compartment. After series production of the M40 and M43 began, these horizontal racks were replaced by universal racks in which 155 mm or 8-inch projectiles were stored vertically. *TACOM LCMC History Office*

Army officers are exploring the first pilot T83 in the first of a series of photos documenting a demonstration of the vehicle upon its official rollout at the Pressed Steel Car Company in Chicago. The barrel of the 155 mm gun is resting on its travel lock. Stenciled on the side of the sponson is "155 mm GUN MOTOR CARRIAGE/ T83-1," the suffix 1 referring to the first pilot vehicle. *Military History Institute*

The canvas muzzle cover on the barrel of the 155 mm gun was a standard accessory for the piece. Note the armored covers for the fuel fillers on the deck over the engine compartment. The eye of a tow cable is visible to the left rear of the driver's cupola. *Military History Institute*

The tailgate and the attached loading ramp are being deployed into their extended positions. The tailgate provided a platform for the crew to stand on while serving the piece, particularly since there was not much floor space in the fighting compartment. The loading ramp provided a means of accessing the platform and the fighting compartment. *Military History Institute*

To the far right on the top carriage of the 155 mm gun is a vertical sheave. This was used in conjunction with a winch cable to retract the gun barrel or haul the barrel into position when necessary. Before May 1945, a modification work order provided for the replacement of the sheave with a retracting eye, but the sheave is sometimes seen in early photos of the T83/M40. *Military History Institute*

Details of the spade and the welded-on teeth along its lower edge are in view in this photo of the rear of the first pilot T83 during a staff briefing. The support for the loading ramp was of bent tubular construction and was shaped like a flattened letter W. Stored upside down on top of the 155 mm gun breech is a loading tray, used for bringing ammunition up to the breech prior to ramming. *Military History Institute*

The second pilot 155 mm Gun Motor Carriage T83, US Army registration number 40193029, featured angled extensions to the rear of the sponsons. This was a design feature carried over to the production 155 mm GMC M40, except with a large, triangular lightening hole in each of the extensions. Two bows are installed to support a tarpaulin. In the background is an 8-inch Howitzer Motor Carriage T84. *Patton Museum*

Following the successful testing of the pilot T83s, the vehicle went into series production in February 1945, with a total of 418 examples being delivered to the Army by the end of December 1945. Shown here is 155 mm GMC T83 registration number 40194776 at the Rock Island Arsenal. In the background is a Medium Tank M4A3(105) HVSS. *Patton Museum*

The 155 mm gun of the second pilot T83 is being fired at an elevation of thirty degrees. The vehicle is equipped with T80 tracks, with chevron treads. The layout of the horizontal volute spring suspension mimicked that of the M4A3E8 medium tank, with three bogie assemblies per side, each with two sets of dual wheels. There were five track-support roller assemblies on each side: two with double rollers with three single rollers. *TACOM LCMC History Office*

At the GMC test ground the first pilot T83 is being subjected to a test to determine the maximum grade it can negotiate. The track it is on is a sixty percent grade, which translates 30.96 degrees. To the right is a test slope of fifty percent grade. Particularly visible from this angle is the square port and roller for the spade cable to the right of the tailgate. *Patton Museum*

The registration number 40194671 is faintly visible on the lower corner of the left side of T83 US serial number 25. Stenciled on the forward end of the sponson is "T83" over "671." Two fold-down crew seats are on the right rear of the fighting compartment. After the first pilot T83, the spade operating cable was moved to the left side of the tailgate. The cable roller to the left of the tailgate hides the cable port in the rear plate of the hull. *National Archives and Records Administration*

In May 1945, the 155 mm Gun Motor Carriage T83 was standardized as the 155 mm Gun Motor Carriage M40. This example, still marked "T83," registration number 40194848 and serial number 200, was photographed at Aberdeen Proving Ground on June 9, 1945. By now, a clamp-type bracket was mounted on each of the trunnion-bearing caps to hold the loading tray. *National Archives and Records Administration*

M40 registration number 40194848 and serial number 200 is viewed from the rear during evaluations at Aberdeen Proving Ground on June 9, 1945. The tailgate, loading ramp, and spade all are lowered. In addition to the travel lock for the 155 mm gun barrel mounted on the glacis, there were two travel locks for the gun carriage; these were steel rods mounted on brackets on the rear of the floor of the fighting compartment, with eyes on the ends that were secured to hooks on the underside of the gun cradle. A close look at this photo reveals that the early-style, non-universal projectile racks were present at the front of the fighting compartment. *National Archives and Records Administration*

The same M40, registration number 40194848, is viewed from the right side with the 155 mm gun elevated, at Aberdeen Proving Ground on June 9, 1945. As mounted in the T83, this gun had a maximum elevation of +55 degrees and a minimum elevation of -5 degrees. The last three numerals of the registration number, 848, were painted on the front of the sponson to the front of "T83."
National Archives and Records Administration

On the same date and place as the preceding photo, M40 40194848 is viewed from the right front. On the right side of the frontal plate of the fighting compartment is a decontamination apparatus. This was not a standard location for this apparatus: according to the T83's on-vehicle equipment list, there was one decontamination apparatus in the assistant driver's compartment and one in the left rear of the fighting compartment. To strengthen the travel lock, there was a steel brace rod on each side, anchored on a bracket on the glacis. A spotlight was to the right front of the assistant driver's cupola. *National Archives and Records Administration*

The same M40 shown in the preceding several photos, 40194848, is viewed from above with the tailgate, loading ramp, and spade raised. Some details of the deck over the engine compartment are visible, including the stored pioneer tools, engine crank, and ventilation grills. On each side of the front of the fighting compartment, to the front of the 155 mm gun shield, are ammunition racks, each holding ten 155 mm projectiles. To the right of the left ammunition rack can be seen the left air cleaner. Note the highly pronounced antislip tread pattern on the inside of the tailgate. *National Archives and Records Administration*

CHAPTER 2
Development of the T30

Much like the M12 was supported by the M30 cargo carrier, with which it shared chassis and hull components, a similar companion vehicle was envisioned for the T83. Not only were military characteristics of the cargo carrier as well as the gun motor carriage laid down in OCM 23098 in early March 1944, the procurement approval of March 23, included provisions for purchase of five cargo carrier pilots along with the gun motor carriages.

The chassis of the T30 was to be identical to that of the T83, however the rear compartment was set up as a large stowage compartment configured specifically to transport ammunition. Initially it was intended that the rear compartment would accommodate readily interchangeable racks set up for either 155 mm or 8-inch ammunition. At the rear of the cargo compartment were two folding seats which were intended to transport crew members. Like the T83, the driver and assistant driver of the T30 were located at the left and right front of the vehicle respectively. The assistant driver's position was equipped with a .50-caliber machine gun supported by a M49 ring mount.

The first pilot model of the T30 was completed along with the pilot T83 on July 28, and was demonstrated at the Pressed Steel Plant alongside the gun motor carriage. The T30 pilot accompanied the T83 pilot to Aberdeen Proving Ground where tests revealed a number of problems.

Although mechanically sound, the arrangement of the cargo compartment was unsatisfactory. In preparing their *First Report on Cargo Carrier T30, First Pilot,* the evaluators at Aberdeen recommended the following corrective actions. Foremost, rather than the then-present racks holding one hundred 155 mm rounds, make the ammunition racks universal, capable of handling "all

types of Field Artillery, large caliber, separate loading ammunition." It was also noted that some sort of mechanical lifting device should be installed to aid in the unloading of projectiles. Arguably the most important change requested related to the exhaust system. During the test operations it was noticed that the floor of the cargo compartment "became exceptionally hot." After installation of thermocouples and operation for two hours with an ambient temperature of 125 degrees, it was found that the projectile temperature would be 180 degrees, slightly above the melting point of TNT, and the floor itself would be 300 degrees—and thus too hot to walk on. To remedy this situation a number of suggestions were made, ranging from increasing insulation to rerouting the exhaust system, which like the T83 was located beneath the floor of the rear compartment.

Accordingly, the T30 was redesigned, becoming the T30E1, and incorporating universal stowage racks permitting the transport of one hundred and two rounds of 155 mm, sixty-six rounds of 8-inch, or thirty-two 240 mm projectiles without modification. A small collapsible ammunition handling crane was installed, as was an air compressor and air brake controls allowing the T30 to tow a M23 ammunition trailer.

However, the utility of a cargo carrier being mechanically identical to the T83 also led to its demise. The power train components of the T30 were also common to the M4 tank, and were accordingly in short supply. Thus, the T30 program was cancelled, and instead the M4C or M4A1C high-speed tractor and M23 ammunition trailer were recommended as support vehicles for the T83.

Civilian and military attendees at the briefing on the first pilot 155 mm Gun Motor Carriage T83 pose for their photo next to the vehicle. Behind the T83 is a Cargo Carrier T30, based on the same chassis as the T83. *Military History Institute*

Since the 155 mm GMC T83 could carry only twenty rounds of ammunition on board, a project was opened to develop a tracked vehicle to operate with the T83 and carry ammunition, cargo, and extra personnel. Hence, the Pressed Steel Car Company received an order to build five pilot Cargo Carriers T30. It was based on the T83 chassis and contained racks for one hundred rounds of 155 mm ammunition, with fifty racks on each side of a central aisle, set at a forty-five-degree angle. Outboard of the racks were compartments for the propellant charges. On each side of the rear door of the ammunition compartment was a crew seat. A ring mount for a .50-caliber machine gun was over the assistant driver's cupola. "TINY" was painted in white on the side of the vehicle. *National Archives and Records Administration*

Ammunition: 100 rds 155 mm , 10 rifle
           grenades, 12 hand grenades,
           14 smoke Bombs M3
Armament: cal .50 AA MG, cal .30 carbine,
          cal .30 rifle M1, smoke mortar 2"
Armor: 2-3/4" (max), $\frac{1}{4}$" (min)
      (4" at nose of final drive housing)
Crew: 4 men
Cruising range: 100 miles
Dimensions: length 271", width 124", height
      121$\frac{1}{2}$"
Engine: Continental R975-C4, 9 cyl., air
     cooled, 395 hp at 2400 rpm (net)

Fuel capacity: 195 gallons
Ground clearance: 17"
Ground pressure: 9.2 psi
Hp to wt. ratio: 13.2 hp per ton
Power train: dry multi disc, syn-
    chronized mechanical constant mesh
    transmission
Speed: 24 mph
Steering: controlled differential
Suspension: horizontal volute spring
Tracks: single pin, center guide, steel
       track T66 (23" wide)
Weight: 73,200 (gross)

The first pilot Cargo Carrier T30 is seen from the right front with a tarpaulin installed over the cargo compartment. The tarpaulin had two window flaps on the front. "CARGO CARRIER/T 30-1" was stenciled toward the front of the sponson but is not very visible. T66 tracks were installed. Note the antenna base and the spotlight to the right front of the assistant driver's cupola.
National Archives and Records Administration

Cargo Carrier T30 pilot number 1 is viewed from the right side. Power was provided by a Continental R975-C4 nine-cylinder air-cooled radial engine. The object on the engine deck to the front of the fighting compartment is a portable storage box with a folded tarpaulin strapped to the top of it. *National Archives and Records Administration*

The first pilot Cargo Carrier T30 is viewed from above, again with a tarpaulin secured over the cargo compartment. The tarpaulin was supported by three bows. Stored on the engine deck are a shovel, sledgehammer, mattock handle, engine starter crank, crowbar, idler-adjustment wrench, axe, and mattock head. *National Archives and Records Administration*

"TINY," the first pilot Cargo Carrier T30, is viewed from the left front without the tarpaulin installed and with the driver's and the assistant driver's hatches open. Like the T83/M40, the T30 had the standard-width final-drive assembly with extended final drives, to sufficiently space the sprockets away from the hull to accommodate the extra width of the hull. Tests found that the T30 was mechanically reliable, but the cargo compartment was unsatisfactory for several reasons, including the difficulty of loading and unloading the ammunition. *TACOM LCMC History Office*

Like the T83/M40, the T30 had front mudguards that were considerably wider than the tracks, extending from the final-drive assembly to the outer face of the sponsons. Also like the T83/M40, there were two headlight assemblies on the glacis, with a small blackout lamp over the service headlight, protected by brush guards with holders for plugs to be inserted in the headlight mounts when the headlights were removed. Next to the left headlight assembly was a horn with its own brush guard. *National Archives and Records Administration*

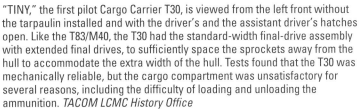

This left-rear photo of the first pilot T30 shows the vehicle with the tarpaulin secured over the cargo compartment. On the rear of the hull was a single door, hinged at the bottom. Welded to each side of the hull are four ladder rungs fabricated from bent rods. Racks for spare track shoes are outboard of the ladder rungs. *National Archives and Records Administration*

The tarpaulin is installed on this Aberdeen Proving Ground photo of a T30 from the rear. The photo is dated September 21, 1944. A sliding bolt was provided on each side of the exterior of the rear door.
National Archives and Records Administration

CHAPTER 3
Development of the T89

After cancellation of the T80 8-in Howitzer Motor Carriage, which had been begun with the premise of using automotive components from the T23 medium tank, the army instead cast an eye toward an 8-in Howitzer Motor Carriage utilizing many power train and suspension components from the M4 medium tank, as had been the case with the 155 mm gun. However, when authorizing the development and production of the T84 in April 1944, Army Service Forces directed that the vehicle be based on the T26E1 medium tank, rather than the M4. However, like all things related to the Pershing tanks, development and production was slowed.

It was under these circumstances that following the successful firing of 200 155 mm rounds from the first T83 pilot at Aberdeen, the gun tube was replaced with an 8-inch howitzer tube, and the corresponding adjustments in recoil action made. Subsequently, seventy-five 8-inch rounds were fired from the vehicle with excellent results.

As a result of these preliminary tests, and in part due to the delays in production of the 8-in Howitzer Motor Carriage T84,

the Ordnance Committee authorized the diversion of the final two T83 pilots for conversion to 8-inch Howitzer Motor Carriage T89. This action was recommended on November 2, 1944, through OCM 25610 and was approved by OCM 25754 on November 16.

The T89 was configured such that the chassis and ammunition stowage was universal and could be used with both 155 mm cannons and 8-inch howitzers. A reversible travel lock was designed which could secure either artillery tube.

The first T89 pilot was completed January 3, 1945, and was shipped to the Lima Tank Depot for equipping with various stowage items, and then to the General Motors Proving Ground in Milford, Michigan, for evaluation by the Maintenance Division. The second pilot was completed on January 9, 1945, and joined the first in Milford. There it was used as reference for the preparation of Technical Manual 9-747.

Subsequently, one of the pilots was sent to the Field Artillery Board for service tests while the other was prepared for overseas shipment.

After the gun of the first pilot 155 mm GMC T83 had test-fired 200 rounds at all possible elevations and traverses with very satisfactory results, the 155 mm gun was removed and an 8-inch Howitzer M1 was substituted for evaluation purposes, again with highly satisfactory results. Thus, the army diverted the final two T83 pilots to 8-inch Howitzer Motor Carriage T89s. Seen here is the first pilot T83 as armed with the 8-inch Howitzer M1. The "BIG SHOT" markings on the rears of the sponsons and the nomenclature stencils on the fronts of the sponsons had been painted over, and these touchups are visible in this photograph in the form of a slightly lighter tone of paint compared to the base color. *Patton Museum*

As seen in an elevated view of the first pilot T83 armed with an 8-inch Howitzer M1, and still wearing the "BIG SHOT" markings on the side, the howitzer barrel was much shorter than that of the 155 mm gun, with a length of 209.59 inches from the muzzle to the rear of the breech, versus 284.4 inches for the 155 mm gun. *National Archives and Records Administration*

The first pilot T83 as rearmed with an 8-inch Howitzer M1 is viewed from the front. The same gun shield as used when a 155 mm gun was mounted is apparently present in unmodified form. The cast cover for the final-drive assembly remained the same width as for the Medium Tank M4A3, but to achieve the width between the sprockets required by the widened hull, each side of the final drives was extended outward. *National Archives and Records Administration*

On November 17, 1944, during evaluations at Aberdeen Proving Ground, crewmen using a standard loading tray are preparing a projectile to be rammed into the 8-inch howitzer mounted on the first pilot T83 chassis. The piece is at 25 degrees elevation, 0 degrees traverse. The tailgate is lowered to form a platform for the crewmen, but the loading ramp is not deployed. *National Archives and Records Administration*

In a second photo of evaluations of the 8-inch howitzer on the first pilot T83 chassis at Aberdeen on November 17, 1944, the crew is using a long, portable tray to load a round into the chamber with the gun at 28 degrees elevation and maximum left traverse. A standard loading tray is lying on the ground to the rear of the spade. Note how the armor had been cut away on the right rear of the vehicle, exposing the manual spade winch to view. *National Archives and Records Administration*

Now, the crew is loading a projectile into the 8-inch howitzer at 0 degrees elevation and maximum left traverse, using the same long, portable loading tray seen in the preceding photograph. It is obvious that loading the piece in this configuration with this loading tray was somewhat problematic. *National Archives and Records Administration*

In a final November 17, 1944, photo of evaluations of the 8-inch howitzer on the first pilot T83 chassis, the crew is preparing to load a projectile with the piece at 0 degrees elevation and 0 degrees traverse. Four men are holding the projectile on a standard loading tray, while the two GIs to the left prepare to begin ramming the projectile up the long tray leading to the breech. The long loading tray had been proposed for production and was undergoing evaluations. *National Archives and Records Administration*

An 8-inch Howitzer Motor Carriage T89 is being emplaced for firing at Aberdeen Proving Ground on April 25, 1945. This may have been one of the pilot T89s, judging by the solid extension plates to the rears of the sponsons, which lack the large, triangular lightening holes associated with the production T89/M43. *National Archives and Records Administration*

The cross-country performance of a T89 is being tested at Aberdeen Proving Ground, Maryland, on April 25, 1945. The 8-inch howitzer barrel is secured in the travel lock, which did not have the X-brace or the outboard steel-rod braces associated with the 155 mm GMC T83/M40. The vehicle is running on T66 tracks. *National Archives and Records Administration*

CHAPTER 4
Further Developments

Seeking increasingly powerful self-propelled artillery, the Ordnance Committee initiated a feasibility study of a heavy mortar emplaced on a T83 chassis on March 15, 1945. One vehicle was converted for evaluation purposes and was designated the 10-inch Mortar Motor Carriage T94 (after May 2, 1946, it was called the 250 mm Mortar Motor Carriage T94). It featured a wooden mock-up of a 10-inch Mortar T5E2 with a crane and a folding apparatus for loading the piece, both of which are shown here in traveling position. The project was cancelled in 1946. *Patton Museum*

Beyond the T83, T89, and T30, consideration was given to a fourth vehicle in the Standard Nomenclature List G-232 family, the T94 250 mm Mortar Motor Carriage. On March 15, 1945, the Ordnance Committee approved the study of the installation of the T5E2 10-inch mortar in a T83 chassis. A T83 was modified with a wooden mock-up of the new weapon, and stowage was configured to accommodate twenty rounds of ammunition, along with the associated handling equipment, and was designated 10-inch Mortar Motor Carriage T94. On May 2, 1946, keeping in line with the new army policy of defining mobile artillery by millimeters, the vehicle was redesignated 250 mm Mortar Motor Carriage T94. However, cancellation of the project had been recommended five months earlier, and no test vehicles were produced beyond the mock-up.

While pleased with the performance of the T83 and T89 during the Zebra Mission, the design, like that of the preceding M12, had some weaknesses. Chief among these was the exposure of the gun crew to air burst artillery rounds and enemy small arms fire and the related lack of close-in defense capabilities.

Maj. Gen. Gladeon M. Barnes, chief of research and engineering in the Ordnance Department, directed that Aberdeen Proving Ground study the installation of secondary weapons and overhead armor protection on the T83.

The second pilot was used for these experiments. Among the installations tried were the equipping of the assistant driver's position with a ball-mount .30 caliber machine gun using Sherman tank components. A pair of pintle-mounted .30 caliber weapons were also installed in the rear corners of the fighting compartment. Mounting these guns on the rear platform, while in the vertical position, was also tried. A test installation of .30 caliber machine guns in the main gun shield, one on each side of the 155 mm was made, but these were deemed of limited utility due to limited traverse.

Test firings were also made of recoilless rifles from the rear fighting compartment machine gun mounts, but it was felt that the back blast from these weapons made them too dangerous to use in such an installation. Thus Aberdeen recommended that should the .30 caliber weapons be deemed inadequate, .50 caliber machine guns be used instead.

Consideration was given to equipping the vehicles with a crew-installable armored enclosure for the fighting compartment. However, it was quickly realized that to make the armor plate light enough to be handled by the crew without lifting devices would necessitate a weak structure.

Ultimately an armored enclosure was designed that, although requiring lifting equipment to install or remove, even provided protection for the crew with the gun in firing position. A full-size wooden mock-up of this armored enclosure was installed on T83 pilot 2, which by this time had been reclassified M40. Ultimately, it was determined that the 2½-ton armored enclosure, while protecting the crew, left the recoil mechanism and equilibrator unprotected, and the modification was deemed unsatisfactory.

The 10-inch Mortar Motor Carriage is viewed from above with the loading apparatus folded for travel. The mock-up of the mortar tube was fabricated from wooden strips; its muzzle is visible to the extreme right. To the far left is the tailgate, raised in the travel position. *Patton Museum*

In a view from above the lowered tailgate of the 10-inch Mortar Motor Carriage T94, a 10-inch mortar round has been placed on the loading apparatus. The upper part of the apparatus has been unfolded and is seen to the upper right. On the left rear of the vehicle is the crane for handling the mortar rounds. *Patton Museum*

As seen in another overhead photograph, the fighting compartment of the 10-inch Mortar Motor Carriage T94 was quite cramped, and included two inward-facing crew seats, storage compartments, and operating gear for the mortar tube. *Patton Museum*

By early 1945, the Army was seeking ways to improve the local-defense capabilities of the 155 mm Gun Motor Carriage M40. Thus, under the direction of Maj. Gen. G.M. Barnes, the Ordnance Research and Development Center, Aberdeen Proving Ground, Maryland, conducted experiments with mounting machine guns and recoilless rifles on M40 serial number 2 and registration number 40193029. This June 23, 1945, photograph shows the left side of the vehicle with a .30-caliber machine on a ball mount similar to those on M4 Sherman bow machine guns, emplaced on the outer part of the gun shield, and a .30-caliber machine gun on a socket mount farther to the rear. *National Archives and Records Administration*

An arrangement of .30-caliber machine guns mirroring those on the left side of the M40 is installed on the right side of the vehicle on June 23, 1945. It was intended that 5,000 rounds of .30-caliber ammunition would be stored on the vehicle. *National Archives and Records Administration*

The test M40 vehicle is viewed from the rear with the four .30-caliber machine guns, two on each side. The socket-mounted machine guns are easily visible: the ones mounted on each side of the gun shield are less easy to make out. The right ball-mounted machine gun was slightly higher than the left one. The photo was dated June 23, 1945. *National Archives and Records Administration*

A Browning M1919 .30-caliber Machine Gun is mounted on the left socket mount of the M40 in a photo taken at Aberdeen Proving Ground on June 28, 1945. The socket mount could hold either the machine gun or the 57 mm Recoilless Rifle. Below the grip and the receiver of the machine gun is the spade winch. *National Archives and Records Administration*

By the time this photo was taken on June 28, 1945, the left ball-mounted .30-caliber machine gun had been dismounted from the gun shield, a steel plug had been welded on the shield where the gun had been mounted, and a 57 mm Recoilless Rifle T15E13 was installed on the left socket mount, at the center of the photo. It was intended that the recoilless rifle normally would be on the right socket mount. Tests of the recoilless rifle on this vehicle indicated that the weapon had an extremely limited field of fire.
National Archives and Records Administration

During the experiments with local-defense weapons on M40 serial number 2, registration number 40193029, two additional socket mounts for .30-caliber machine guns were welded to the upper corners of the tailgate, as seen in a June 28, 1945, photograph at Aberdeen Proving Ground. These two guns had an excellent field of fire to the rear, but they had to be dismounted before the tailgate could be lowered and used as a loading platform.
National Archives and Records Administration

The defensive armaments project for the M40 undertaken at Aberdeen Proving Ground in 1945 also included the installation of a .30-caliber ball-mount bow machine gun in the assistant driver's position. This weapon, the same type of ball mount used on M4 Sherman Medium Tanks, was found during tests to be an effective defensive weapon. This photo was taken at Aberdeen Proving Ground on July 26, 1945, the same date the Army cancelled the defensive-armaments project for the M40.
National Archives and Records Administration

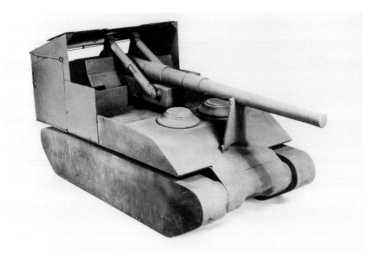

Toward the end of World War II, the Army undertook experiments to improve the protection for the gun crew of the M40. This 1/8 scale model, photographed at Aberdeen Proving Ground on July 4, 1945, shows an M40 with an armored enclosure over the fighting compartment. This enclosure, also referred to as a cab, was intended to protect the crew from enemy small-arms fire and fragments from air-burst artillery shells. The enclosure is shown in travel position, with frontal flaps swung back over the roof. *National Archives and Records Administration*

The cab armor is extended in this photograph. The armor, when extended in this manner, did not in any way impede the traverse or elevation of the gun. Nevertheless, tests of the vehicle at Aberdeen Proving Ground in 1945, indicated that the armored cab was unsatisfactory and, if the Army decided that improved crew protection for the M40 was necessary, it was preferable to redesign the upper hull and the gun mount toward that end. *National Archives and Records Administration*

As was the case with Aberdeen Proving Ground's experiments with mounting machine guns and a recoilless rifle on an M40, the vehicle used for the armored-cab experiments (Project 6-2-61-3) was serial number 2, registration number 40193029, as shown in a November 6, 1945, photograph. The cab enclosure was a mockup built of 3/4-inch plywood on a frame made of 2x4 lumber. Here, the front armor is folded back. The frame supporting the cab armor had vertical stakes that fit into pockets attached to the side armor of the fighting compartment. *National Archives and Records Administration*

In this top right view of the M40 with cab armor, the frontal plates are folded back on the cab roof. Three different materials were considered for the armored cab: 7/8-inch Duraluminum, 1/2-inch homgenous or face-hardened armor plate, and 3/4-inch homogenous or face-hardened armor plate. Weights of the cabs would have ranged from 3,151 pounds for the Duraluminum to 5,134 pounds for the 3/4-inch armor. The Ballistic Research Laboratory conducted studies on the amount of protection each material would provide. *National Archives and Records Administration*

The armored cab would not have provided cover from fragments or projectiles from the rear of the vehicle, but the hinged extensions at the rear of the armor, shown extended here, would have offered protection to crewmen on the loading ramp from above and to the sides. *National Archives and Records Administration*

This November 6, 1945, photograph from Aberdeen Proving Ground depicts the armored cab with the rear extensions folded. If the armored cab had gone into production, it would have been necessary to use overhead hoists to lift the components of the cab onto the vehicle or to remove them. *National Archives and Records Administration*

The M40 with the armored cab mockup installed is viewed from the right side with the hinged armor panels extended. One of the main criticisms of the armored cab was that it offered no protection to the equilibrators, which were quite vulnerable to damage from shell fragments and bullets. *National Archives and Records Administration*

The mockup of the armored cab is viewed from the rear at Aberdeen Proving Ground on November 6, 1945. The hinged armor plates are in their extended positions. *National Archives and Records Administration*

This 155 mm Gun Motor Carriage M40 has been outfitted with a deep-fording kit. Air-intake trunks are installed over the engine compartment on both sides of the 155 mm gun, and an exhaust trunk is attached to the rear of the hull. *Patton Museum*

A 155 mm GMC M40 with a deep-fording kit installed is negotiating a body of water during a test run. Latches for securing the left air-intake trunk are visible on the bottom of the outboard side of that trunk. *Patton Museum*

CHAPTER 5

The M40 and M43 in Service

Following the previously discussed December 1944 meeting of interested parties concerning the refinement of the T83, it was intended to return pilot number 3 to Pressed Steel Car for use as a production reference. However, instead the vehicle was prepared for overseas shipment as part of the Zebra Mission.

This technical mission was intended to evaluate the performance of the army's new ordnance material in Europe, especially the new T26E3 tank (twenty examples), but also included the T83 pilot 3 and one of the T89 pilots. Upon arrival in Europe, the T83 and T89 were assigned to the 991st Field Artillery Battalion, which was then using the M12.

That unit, in order to achieve uniformity of caliber, replaced the 8-inch tube of the T89 with a M1A1 155 mm tube. Later, during the siege of Cologne, this vehicle had the distinction of being the first piece to fire on German positions within the city. Ultimately, the 8-inch tube was reinstalled on the T89, and the vehicle deployed in that configuration as well.

Limited procurement of the T83 had been initiated by OCM 24413 on July 3, 1944, even before the first pilot was delivered. Initially, 304 T83s and T30s were to have been ordered. This was subsequently changed to 600 T83 vehicles on production order T-17231, and a further sixteen on T-21692.

Series production of these vehicles began with the shipment of a single example in February 1945, followed by sixty in March, one hundred in April, and monthly shipments of seventy-five in April and May. Production of the T83 was stopped after 418 examples were completed, reflecting the Allied victory.

Production of the T89 was a bit more problematic. In April 1945, a contract was issued to Pressed Steel for 576 of the 8-inch howitzer motor carriages as a Limited Procurement type on order T-22312. However, subsequent to the cessation of hostilities, the order was cancelled after only twenty-four of the vehicles had been produced. Lima Tank Depot, operating under production order T-22784, converted a further twenty-four of the 418 T83s built by Pressed Steel into T89 configuration. This resulted in the army having available forty-eight T89 vehicles and 394 T83 vehicles.

While none of these, but for the previously mentioned single examples of T83 and T89, saw combat in World War II, these vehicles would form the core of America's post-World War II heavy field artillery. The T83 had been standardized as the M40 in May 1945, and the T89 was standardized as the M43 by OCM29666 on November 8, 1945.

With the outbreak of war in Korea, both types were used extensively in combat. The 204th and 937th Field Artillery Battalions were deployed with the M40, with the M43 being fielded by the 987th Field Artillery Battalion. Both types were used with considerable success, solidifying the concept of self-propelled heavy artillery with strategists. After the Korean cease-fire the US Army replaced both types with fully enclosed self-propelled guns. Some M40s were supplied to Great Britain under the Mutual Defense Assistance Program (MDAP) in two batches totaling twenty-seven vehicles between 1953 and 1955. The Royal Artillery used the M40 for about a decade. Others were sent to France, who used the vehicles as late as 1972.

One each of the pilot T83s and T89s were shipped to Europe with Zebra Mission in time to see action with the 991st Field Artillery Battalion in the final weeks of World War II in the Europena Theater of Operations (ETO). That battalion soon replaced the 8-inch howitzer on the T89 with a 155 mm gun. One of those vehicles is seen here in a firing position next to a wrecked Junkers Ju 87 Stuka at a recently captured Luftwaffe base in the First US Army sector near Burbach, Germany. The gun on this vehicle reportedly was a 155 mm Gun M1A1. A number stenciled in white, presumably the US Army registration number, is faintly visible on the side of the vehicle, but only the last two digits, 74, are readable.
National Archives and Records Administration

The crew of the T83 assigned to the 991st Field Artillery Battalion in Germany, pauses for their photo between firing on German positions in the distance. A rammer staff is lying to the rear of the left crewman on the tailgate, and a 155 mm projectile is on the right side of the tailgate. A bazooka is resting atop the storage compartments on the right side of the fighting compartment. *Patton Museum*

In what appears to be a companion photo to the preceding image, the converted T89 with a 155 mm Gun M1A1 is in a firing position on the outskirts of Cologne, Germany, in 1945. The center man on the tailgate has the firing lanyard in his hand, ready to pull it to fire the piece. On top of the left side of the fighting compartment is the loading rack. *Patton Museum*

The original caption for this photograph of an 8-inch Howitzer Motor Carriage M43, as the T89 had been designated when standardized in November 1945, identifies the subject as the "first self-propelled gun ever to be brought on the Camp McCoy reservation" in Wisconsin on February 8, 1951. It had just arrived there by railroad flatcar and was being driven off a platform. A tarpaulin was secured over the fighting compartment to keep out the elements. Several sections of spare tracks are stored on the glacis. *National Archives and Records Administration*

On the day after the preceding photo was taken, an 8-inch Howitzer Motor Carriage M43 is being prepared for firing at Camp McCoy, Wisconsin, on February 9, 1951. The US Army registration number, 40194871, is painted in white on the lower rear of the side of the hull, and several other stencils, including inspection markings, are present on the side of the vehicle. Both of the cupola hatches are open. *National Archives and Records Administration*

Troops are preparing 8-inch Howitzer Motor Carriage M43 registration number 40222488 for unloading from a flatcar at Camp Polk, Louisiana. This was one of two M43s that arrived there from the Lima Ordnance Depot, Ohio, in late April or early March 1951, and were assigned to the 190th Field Artillery Group. Unlike several of the T89s and M43s seen in earlier photos, this example had the additional steel-rod braces for the travel lock. *National Archives and Records Administration*

This is the first of a series of photos of 155 mm GMC M40s of the 937th Field Artillery Battalion, an Arkansas National Guard unit, emplaced in excavated firing positions outside of Cheorwon, South Korea, on April 8–9, 1951. The closest vehicle is registration number 40205201. The M40 in the right background has the nickname "COURAGEOUS CONFEDERATE" painted on the side. An Arkansas state flag is planted to the front of the closest M40. Partially visible in the background are an M4 high-speed tractor and a half-track with a quad .50-caliber gun mount. *National Archives and Records Administration*

The same two M40s of the 937th Field Artillery Battalion seen in the preceding photo are viewed at the same firing position from the opposite direction on April 8, 1951. "COURAGEOUS CONFEDERATE" is in the closest emplacement; its registration number is visible: 40194684. To the right rear of this M40 is an M4 high-speed tractor. Next in line is M40 40205201. Farther down the line in the left background are two more M40s in prepared positions. The farthest M40 has its 155 mm gun set at approximately maximum elevation. *National Archives and Records Administration*

M40 registration number 40205201of the 937th Field Artillery Battalion, Arkansas National Guard, is viewed from the front in its excavated firing position outside of Cheorwon on April 9, 1951. Two sections of three spare track links are stored on the glacis, and the travel lock has the extra steel-rod braces to the sides. The jeep to the left rear of the M40 has "THE ASSOCIATED PRESS" marked on the bottom of the windshield frame. *National Archives and Records Administration*

The M40s of the 937th Field Artillery Battalion are shelling Communist positions at Cheorwon on the night of April 8, 1951. The second M40 in line has the nickname "AITA'S ANKIES" painted on its side. Lying on the ground to the right rear of the closer M40 is a row of 155 mm projectiles.
National Archives and Records Administration

"COURAGEOUS CONFEDERATE," M40 registration number 40194684, of the 937th Field Artillery Battalion, seen at a distance in some of the preceding images, is viewed close-up during the April 9, 1951 shelling of Communist positions at Cheorwon, Korea. A small Confederate battle flag is attached to the whip antenna. A bore-cleaning brush with a handle apparently improvised from a tree branch is leaning against the left rear of the vehicle. *National Archives and Records Administration*

Crewmen are preparing "AITA'S ANKIES" in the background and M40 nicknamed "BETTY LOU," registration number 40205196, foreground, for firing at a prepared site outside of Cheorwon, Korea, on April 9, 1951. The site was just 300 yards behind the front lines, five miles south of the Imjin River, and the fire mission, conducted by the 937th Field Artillery Battalion, was in support of the 24th Regiment. *National Archives and Records Administration*

M40s of the 937th Field Artillery Battalion fire on Communist forces concentrated at Cheorwon, Korea, on the night of April 9, 1951. The extreme elevation of several of the guns is evidence of the very close ranges at which they were firing. *National Archives and Records Administration*

After an all-day fire mission on April 13, 1951, an M40 crewman has shimmied out to the end of the 155 mm gun barrel with a bucket of water, ready to pour it on the bore-cleaning brush at the end of the staff the crewmen to the rear of the vehicle are pushing on. This vehicle was registration number 40205140, serving with the 204th Field Artillery Battalion. The trailer in the foreground has markings for Battery A, 204th FAB. *National Archives and Records Administration*

M40s of the 204th Field Artillery Battalion shell Chinese Communist positions north of Seoul on the night of April 26, 1951. Four M40s are visible in this photograph, and they all are firing more or less in unison. *National Archives and Records Administration*

The crew of an M40 of the 937th Field Artillery Battalion pose for a group portrait at battalion headquarters on the central front in Korea on May 13, 1951. This was an Arkansas National Guard unit, and most of the crewmen were from the state, but a few were from states such as New York, Iowa, Alabama, and North Carolina. All but the last digit of the M40's registration number is visible: 4020519. To the far left is a grease can with pump and hose. *National Archives and Records Administration*

Seen previously in several photos from April 1951, "AITA'S ANKIES," registration number 40194754, of Section 3, Battery A, 937th Field Artillery Battalion, is shelling communist positions near Yanggu, Korea, on June 26, 1951. The 155 mm gun has just fired a shot and is in full recoil. At the time this photo was taken, this battery had been attached temporarily to the 96th Field Artillery Battalion. *National Archives and Records Administration*

During a visit to the frontlines in Korea on April 11, 1951, Secretary of the Army Frank Pace Jr., standing on the right side of the tailgate of a 155 mm Gun Motor Carriage M40, is grasping the firing lanyard of the gun, ready to send a shot to a Communist position. The nickname "BETTY JO" is painted in white on the gun barrel. Below the feet of the crewman to the left is stenciled "937 F," the symbol for the unit the vehicle was assigned to, the 937th Field Artillery Battalion. Another M40 is in the right background. Although difficult to discern in the shadows, in the front right corner of the fighting compartment is a late-type, universal projectile rack for storing 155 mm or 8-inch ammunition. *National Archives and Records Administration*

Corporal Billy Bedwell of Linton, Indiana, the number 2 crewman of an M40 assigned to the 3rd Gun Section, 937th Field Artillery Battalion, inserts fuzes into 155 mm projectiles preparatory to the shelling of Communist forces near Yanggu, Korea, on June 25, 1951. The plugs with rings were first unscrewed from the fuze sockets. *National Archives and Records Administration*

Members of the 2nd Section, Battery A, 937th Field Artillery Battalion, temporarily attached to the 96th Field Artillery Battalion, are preparing to emplace a 155 mm GMC M40, registration number 40194767, outside of Yanggu, Korea, on June 26, 1951. In the left background is a towed 8-inch howitzer. *National Archives and Records Administration*

The same M40 shown in the preceding photograph, registration number 40194767, has been emplaced at a site near Yanggu, Korea, on June 26, 1951, and is firing a shot at Chinese Communist forces. Worthy of notice are the retainer chains on each side of the tailgate, seen on some M40s by this time period, and the brackets for storing a standard ammunition tray on top of the trunnion-bearing caps. A bore-swabbing brush in a bucket is to the left of the tailgate. *National Archives and Records Administration*

The crew of the previously seen "AITA'S ANKIES," registration number 40194754, cover their ears as the 155 mm gun fires a shot at an enemy position outside of Yanggu, Korea, on June 30, 1951. The vehicle and crew were part of Section 2, Battery A, 937th Field Artillery Battalion, assigned to the 96th Field Artillery Battalion. *National Archives and Records Administration*

"AITA'S ANKIES" fires another shot at Communist forces near Yanggu on June 30, 1951. This was the daytime firing position for this battery; at night, the unit moved to a different firing site. To the right rear of the loading ramp aft of the tailgate is a large supply of 155 mm projectiles. *National Archives and Records Administration*

"CHARMING CYNTHIA" was another one of the 155 mm GMC M40s of the 937th Field Artillery Battalion in Korea. Posing with the vehicle is crewman Sgt. Robert Pesterfield, who is pointing to his nickname on the roster of "Bashful Bachelors" painted on the side of the M40: "Rapid Robert." Sgt. Pesterfield said of this self-propelled gun, "She's loud, but she sure sings a sweet song."
National Archives and Records Administration

Members of Battery C, 937th Field Artillery Battalion, prepare to load a projectile into the 155 mm gun of an M40 on July 5, 1951, while supporting the 24th US Infantry Division. Painted on the projectile is "Whistler's Mother." The second man from the left is a Korean volunteer soldier; he is holding a propellant charge. *National Archives and Records Administration*

The 155 mm gun of the M40 nicknamed "AITA'S ANKIES" engages in a direct-fire mission against a Communist position on Hill 773 near Yanggu on August 2, 1951. In the foreground are packing tubes for 155 mm propellant charges. The chevron-shaped treads are immediately visible on the T80 tracks.
National Archives and Records Administration

An M40 pounds away at a Chinese Communist position near Mago-ri, Korea, on August 21, 1951. A crewman crouching to the rear of the loading ramp is clutching a rammer staff. On the ground to the far left to the front of the crewman who is plugging his ears is a 155 mm projectile in a standard loading tray, ready to be brought up the breech of the piece. Note the rectangular opening in the assistant driver's hatch where the periscope has been removed. *National Archives and Records Administration*

The crew of a 155 mm GMC M40 of Battery C, 204th Field Artillery Battalion, fires across the Imjin River at enemy forces west of Yonchon, Korea, on September 27, 1951. The vehicle and crew were attached to the 1st Cavalry Division. The raised, wavy pattern of the anti-slip tread on the tailgate is visible from this angle. To the left of the left trunnion-bearing cap is a Panoramic Telescope M12.
National Archives and Records Administration

In a snow-covered clearing on the west-central front of Korea, near the village of Munema, an M40 and crew of Section 4, Battery B, 937th Field Artillery Battalion, carry out a nighttime fire mission in general support of the 25th US Infantry Division on November 25, 1951. The vehicle is seen from the rear as it fires a shot. *National Archives and Records Administration*

"BIG BRUISER," an M40 assigned to Battery B, 937th Field Artillery Battalion, carried on that battalion's tradition in Korea of painting large nicknames on the sides of the M40s, with the words of the nickname sharing one large, common first letter. Another M40, with a similarly constituted but mostly hidden nickname, is in the background, visible to the rear of "BIG BRUISER." These vehicles were acting in support of the 9th Infantry Regiment, 2nd Infantry Division. *National Archives and Records Administration*

A 155 mm GMC M40 assigned to Battery B, 937th Field Artillery Battalion, conducts a fire-support mission for the 9th Infantry Regiment, 2nd Infantry Division, in Korea on January 8, 1952. A small white star insignia is on each side of the rear of the hull. *National Archives and Records Administration*

Members of an M40 crew of Battery B, 937th Field Artillery Battalion, are ramming a 155 mm projectile into the gun on January 20, 1952. To the rear of the vertical slot in the armored shield to the right of the gun is an Elbow Telescope M16A1F, below which is the operating handle for the breech block. The staff sergeant standing on the right side of the fighting compartment has his right foot in the stirrup of the locking lever for the elevation mechanism. *National Archives and Records Administration*

The crewman to the left is affixing a primer to the breech block of the 155 mm gun of an M40 assigned to Battery B, 937th Field Artillery Battalion, on January 20, 1952. The primer was inserted in the Firing Lock M17. When the crewman to the right pulled the lanyard in his hand, it actuated the trigger on the firing lock, detonating the primer and the propellant charge, thus firing the projectile. Visible in the left front corner of the fighting compartment are vertically-stored projectiles in packing tubes, indicative of the later-style universal shell racks. *National Archives and Records Administration*

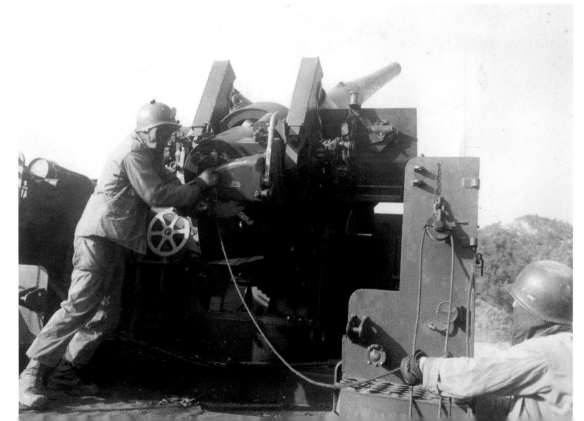

"BELLERN' BABY," M40 registration number 40205167, serving with the 937th Field Artillery Battalion, fires a 155 mm shell destined for a target fifteen miles away on January 20, 1952. Several women's names, presumably those of wives or girlfriends of crew members, are painted in white on the vehicle, including, from rear forward, "DELORES/BRIGHT," "ETHELREOR/BURNETT," and "GLADYS."
National Archives and Records Administration

On February 20, 1952, Lt. Col. James DeVaughn and Capt. Lawrence Dewberry inspect a 155 mm Gun Motor Carriage M40 that recently arrived at the Georgia Military District. The stencils on the side of the vehicle include instruction on servicing that has been done to the vehicle and servicing still to be done. *National Archives and Records Administration*

The "937 FA" marking indicating the 937th Field Artillery Battalion is visible on the left rear of this M40 seen firing at Communist forces from an outpost of the 2nd US Infantry Division on February 21, 1952. Note the rammer staff leaning against the right side of the tailgate and the shorter swabbing-brush handle leaning against the left side of the tailgate. *National Archives and Records Administration*

The same M40 shown in the preceding photo is viewed from a closer perspective as it shells an enemy position on February 21, 1952. The marking "A 26" is visible on the right rear of the vehicle, signifying Battery A and the 26th vehicle in the order of march for the battalion. *National Archives and Records Administration*

On March 13, 1952, GIs of Battery B, 937th Field Artillery Battalion, are loading the 155 mm gun on an M40. The projectile is already in the chamber of the gun, and a staff sergeant on the tailgate is holding the loading tray on which the crewmen brought the projectile to the breech for ramming. On the left side of the tailgate, a crewman is about to insert a bagged propellant charge into the breech.
National Archives and Records Administration

One of the M40s of the 937th Field Artillery Battalion of the 2nd US Infantry Division has just sent a 155 mm projectile on its way to the enemy on March 13, 1952. A two-word nickname sharing a large, common first letter, in the common style of the 937th, is visible, but only the upper word, "Billing's," is discernibile. *National Archives and Records Administration*

An 8-inch Howitzer Motor Carriage M43 fires at Chinese Communist forces north of Yonchon on May 6, 1952. The nickname "PERSUADERS" is stenciled on the howitzer barrel. Some of the crewmen have opened their mouths at the moment of firing, to reduce the pressure of the blast concussion on their eardrums. *Rock Island Arsenal Museum*

A wrecker is being employed to remove the barrel of a 155 mm gun from its mount on an M40 assigned to Battery B, 204th Field Artillery Battalion, at a base in Korea on June 28, 1952. The M40 was registration number 40194831. In the background is another M40 with a tarpaulin over the fighting compartment and extending over the tailgate. *National Archives and Records Administration*

An M43 assigned to Battery A, 17th Field Artillery Battalion, lays down 8-inch fire in support of elements of the 2nd US Infantry Division fighting on "Old Baldy," as Hill 266 in west-central Korea was known, on August 22, 1952. Note the retracting eye mounted on the top carriage between the equilibrators. *National Archives and Records Administration*

M40 registration 40194727 of Battery C, 937th Field Artillery Battalion, is emplaced in a sandbagged revetment at a fire base in Korea on January 5, 1953. An unusually large star insignia is on the side of the vehicle. A nickname beginning with the letter C is also on the hull but is indistinct. The revetments were outfitted with heated bunkers and facilities for storing ammunition.
National Archives and Records Administration

At the same fire base shown in the preceding photograph, an M40 attached to the 3rd Section of Battery C, 937th Field Artillery Battalion, is being prepared for the next fire mission. A number of 155 mm projectiles are stored on their bases along the sandbagged revetment to the right. To the far right is a sign that reads "3rd SECTION." *National Archives and Records Administration*

A delegation of Greek military officers is aboard a 155 mm GMC M40 at a demonstration of US Army firepower at a base in West Germany on April 29, 1953. The registration number to the rear of the star insignia is 40194910. The vehicle is in impeccable condition and is fitted with T80 tracks. *National Archives and Records Administration*

The crew of M40 registration number 40194940 of Battery C, 393rd Field Artillery Battalion, readies the vehicle for firing during Command Post Exercise (CPX) Monte Carlo, on September 13, 1953. The battalion was stationed at that time at Hersfeld, West Germany. The nickname "Catastrophe" is painted on the sponson above the registration number, and a round insignia is farther aft on the sponson, to the rear of the man standing next to the vehicle. *National Archives and Records Administration*

Sgt. Charles Lewis of Mena, Arkansas, a member of Battery A, 933rd Field Artillery Battalion, stands on the rim of the driver's cupola of an M40 during a summer encampment at Camp Chaffee, Arkansas, on July 23, 1954. Spare tracks on the glacis are stored in racks with deep cutouts to hold the track pins. The tracks on this vehicle are the postwar T84 type with rubber chevron treads. *National Archives and Records Administration*

Two crewmen of Battery A, 512th Field Artillery Battalion, take a break on a 155 mm Gun Motor Carriage M40 at Camp Drake, Japan, on June 24, 1955. The registration number, 4019478, has a large gap between the 9 and the 4. On the left front mudguard is the vehicle's order-of-march number, 14. A roll of camouflage netting is on the glacis. *National Archives and Records Administration*

Members of Battery A, 593rd Field Artillery Battalion, are training with their 8-inch Howitzer Motor Carriage M43, registration number 40205209, at Grafenwohr, West Germany, on August 10, 1955. Some M43s and M40s during this period had the cost of the vehicle marked on the side, this one has "COST – $185,000" painted to the front of the star insignia. A close examination of the photo reveals a modification: an exhaust tailpipe on the right rear of the engine deck. There was a similar pipe on the left side, and these replaced the exhausts that formerly had run beneath the fighting compartment.
National Archives and Records Administration

On the same date as the preceding photo at Grafenwohr, the crew of 8-inch Howitzer Motor Carriage (HMC) M43 registration number 40205152 loads their piece during a training exercise. They were serving with Battery A, 593rd Field Artillery Battalion. The man in the left foreground is getting the rammer out of the way, having just assisted in ramming the projectile into the chamber, while a crewman on the tailgate is about to shove a bagged propellant charge into the chamber of the howitzer.
National Archives and Records Administration

The same 8-inch HMC M43 featured in the preceding photograph, registration number 40205152, is viewed from the left side as several crewmen lean into a rammer staff to insert a projectile into the chamber. To the side of the rear of the vehicle is an ammunition trailer. Several projectiles and propellant packing tubes are on the ground to the rear of the trailer. *National Archives and Records Administration*

Members of an M43 crew of Battery A, 593rd Field Artillery Battalion, are preparing 8-inch howitzer rounds for firing at the Grafenwohr Training Area on August 10, 1955. These men were engaged in tests to determine their and their equipment's battle-readiness. Two men to the right are assembling a rammer staff; behind one of them is a loading tray with an 8-inch projectile resting on it. The crewmen to the left are readying projectiles, including inserting fuzes. *National Archives and Records Administration*

The barrel of the 8-inch howitzer of M43 registration number 40205152 of Battery A, 593rd Field Artillery Battalion, is in recoil after firing a round during proficiency tests at the Grafenwohr Training Area in West Germany, on August 10, 1955. The crew's rifles and carbines are stacked to the side of the vehicle. *National Archives and Records Administration*

Another field artillery battalion that trained at Grafenwohr in August 1955, was the 18th. Here, men of Battery A of the 18th conduct a practice fire mission with their 155 mm Gun Motor Carriage M40 on August 11 in preparation for their proficiency tests. Some of the crewmen are ramming a projectile into the chamber of the gun while another crewman to the rear of the tailgate is ready with a bagged propellant charge. *National Archives and Records Administration*

The same M40 shown in the preceding photograph, registration number 40194807, is viewed from the opposite side as the crew rams a projectile into the 155 mm gun. Projectiles and propellant packing cases are to the left side of the vehicle. The nickname "AGGRESSOR" was stenciled on both sides of the 155 mm gun barrel. *National Archives and Records Administration*

This 8-inch Howitzer Motor Carriage M43 was photographed at an unidentified base in Germany during August 1955. A good view is available of the right exhaust pipe on the rear of the engine deck: a modification found on some M43s and M40s in the mid-1950s. *Verne W. Kindschi*

The same M43 featured in the preceding photo, registration number 40222485, is seen from a different angle. There are extensive paint touch ups on this vehicle in several different shades of Olive Drab. Bright red paint has been applied to the idler hubcap. *Verne W. Kindschi*

A 155 mm Gun Motor Carriage M40 preserved at the US Army Artillery Museum, Ft. Sill, Oklahoma, is viewed from the left front. This example is equipped with T80 tracks. Many of the small, original parts are present, from the steel-rod braces to the sides of the travel lock to the brush guards and the small clamp for holding a tow cable on the left front of the final-drive assembly, but the horn and the headlights have been removed from their mounts on the glacis.

Details of the bolted-on track guides, the track connectors, and the left sprocket assembly are in view. The sprocket assembly is part number D47366, the variant in which the ends of the tabs of the sprocket rims that are bolted to the sprocket drum are rounded rather than squared.

The glacis of an M40 is viewed from the left front, with an emphasis on the brush guards for the left headlight assembly (which is not present) and the horn. To the front of the brush guard for the horn is the bracket for the left steel-rod brace for the travel lock. This bracket was a welded structure with a U-bolt on top for attaching the brace.

The front left horizontal volute spring suspension (HVSS) bogie assembly is depicted. Each unit had two paired bogie wheels with rubber tires, mounted on suspension arms, with a horizontal volute spring assembly between them and a horizontal shock absorber at the top, linking the upper extensions of the suspension arms.

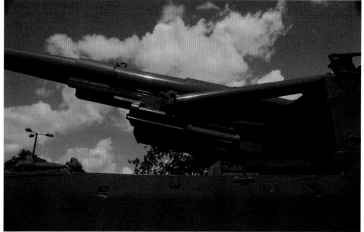

Elements of the 155 mm gun barrel, the recoil slide, and the gun cradle are seen from the left side of the M40. The cradle formed a structure for supporting the gun and housing the recoil and recuperation cylinders, as well as a surface for the gun to slide on during recoil and recuperation. At the center of the photo is the coupling of the left equilibrator to the gun cradle. The cylinders on the side of the cradle below that coupling are the variable recoil housing (upper) and the replenisher assembly (below). Visible above the sleeve at the front of the gun slide is a ring, used for retracting and hauling out the gun barrel using a winch cable.

In a left-rear view of the M40, the roller for the winch cable that operated the spade is on the left rear of the vehicle. One end of the cable was attached to the winch inside the left rear corner of the fighting compartment, with the remainder of the cable routed over the roller and around pulleys on the corners of the spade and the right rear of the hull.

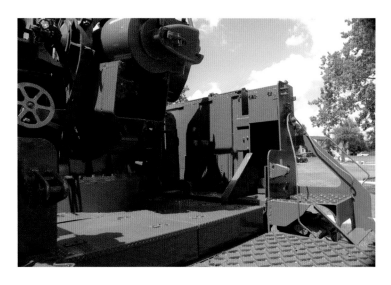

The wavy, non-slip treads on the tailgate were tack-welded in place. The pronged objects protruding through the floor of the tailgate are the locking links for the spade. Stowed underneath the tailgate is the loading platform, the support for which is in the lowered position.

Visible inside the open rear end of the gun cradle are, left, the rear of the recoil piston assembly, and to the right, the rear of the counterrecoil piston over the rear of the recuperator assembly. Below the cradle are the elevating sector and the drum-shaped base of the gun mount. On the right side of the fighting compartment were storage compartments for eight powder charges and also for fuzes.

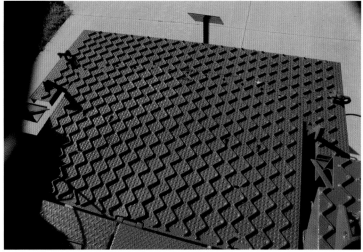

The breech, the rear of the gun cradle, and the trunnion-bearing caps, to which the rears of the equilibrators are attached, are seen from the left rear of an M40. Attached to the tops of the trunnion-bearing caps are racks or holders for storing a loading tray. At the bottom of the photo is a grab handle.

The tailgate of the M40 has an interesting structure, consisting of a steel plate with a diamond tread pattern, over which has been painstakingly tack-welded a series of wavy or zig-zagging steel strips, forming a very pronounced non-slip surface. The small platforms on the rear of the hull to the sides of the tailgates also have these wavy strips, as seen to the lower right.

Details of the 155 mm gun breech and carriage, the rear of the gun shield, and the fighting compartment are in view. To the left side of the gun carriage is the traversing hand wheel; the elevating hand wheel is visible in profile on the right side of the carriage. On each side of the front of the fighting compartment is an early-type, horizontal rack for ten 155 mm projectiles, each rack holding the projectiles two abreast by five in height. After the end of World War II, these racks were replaced by universal racks for storing vertically either 155 mm or 8-inch projectiles. On the left rear of the fighting compartment is the manual winch for operating the spade.

Inside the left rear corner of the fighting compartment of the M40 is a manual winch for raising and lowering the spade, minus its hand crank. Farther forward on the left side of the fighting compartment are compartments for storing twelve bagged propellant charges.

In a view of the rear of the breech of the 155 mm gun of an M40, the firing mechanism is mounted on the center of the breech. At the lower center is the traversing hand wheel, above which are the mounts for the Panoramic Telescope M12 and the separate Telescope M69E1.

The manual spade winch in the left rear of an M40 is viewed from the front. The gearbox is to the left and the cable drum to the right. The winch also operated the tailgate and loading ramp, which were linked to the spade.

The traversing hand wheel and, to the lower front of it, the associated rack and pinion, are viewed close-up. To the front and left of the hand wheel is the left projectile rack, which is in a deteriorated condition. Several of the storage tubes of the rack are missing, and the perforated plate that acted to retain the projectiles in their tubes is corroded at the bottom.

The perforated retainer plate for the left projectile rack, to the left, and the traversing hand wheel are viewed from a different angle. The small, ball-shaped object above and to the front of the hand wheel was part of the locking mechanism for the traversing wheel. The box at the upper center was the storage case for the panoramic telescope.

The small platform with non-slip tread on the left rear of the hull of the M40 is viewed from the center rear of the fighting compartment. The bracket-shaped object above the front of the platform, at the center of the photo, formed the latch bracket for the left locking link of the spade, seen protruding through the tailgate to the left.

Adjacent to the left trunnion of the 155 mm gun of the M40 are two telescope mounts. The one to the left, in line with the trunnion, is the Telescope Mount M18A1, for the Panoramic Telescope M12 (not mounted in this photo). To the rear of that mount is the T122 mount for the Telescope M69E1, also not mounted.

On the right side of the 155 mm gun carriage are the elevating hand wheel and gearbox. The hollow tube below the hand wheel, with a rod and stirrup mounted on the bottom of it, is the braking lever for the elevating mechanism.

To the right side of the right trunnion of the 155 mm gun are the Mount M71 for a Telescope M16A1F, below which is a Quadrant Mount M1. Below these mounts are the elevation hand wheel, gear box, and braking lever. To the upper right is the right side of the gun shield, with a vertical slot to accommodate the Telescope M16A1F.

The elevating hand wheel, gearbox, and braking lever are viewed from a different perspective in the fighting compartment of an M40. Also in view are the right projectile rack (with the bottoms of some of the storage tube rusted out) and storage compartments for fuses and bagged propellant charges.

The same elements shown in the preceding photograph are seen from a slightly different angle, looking more downward.

The doors on top of the propellant-charge compartments on the right side of the fighting compartment of an M40 are viewed from the rear. Each door had two hinges on the outer side and a latch handle on the inner side. A weld bead is present between the two doors, presumably to immobilize the doors when the vehicle was retired from active service.

The 155 mm Gun Motor Carriage M40 is viewed from the right rear, showing details of the tailgate and, to the lower left, the support for the loading platform. Note the three grab handles on the rear edge of the loading platform, which is slid into its travel position.

In the rear of the fighting compartment of the M40 beneath four removable diamond-tread floor plates equipped with grab handles were removable toolboxes. At the top of the photo is the lowered tailgate.

The spade of an M40 is seen from the right side while in its lowered position. Although tests indicated that the 155 mm gun of the M40 could be safely fired from all positions without the spade engaged, it was prudent to dig in the spade before firing the piece.

The 155 mm Gun Motor Carriage M40 is viewed from the right rear. On the right side of the breechblock is the curved handle for operating the breechblock, acting to lock and unlock the unit and serving as a lever for swinging it open.

The same 155 mm Gun Motor Carriage M40 is observed from the right front. It can be seen how the travel lock formed an impediment to the driver's line of sight through the vision blocks of the cupola toward the right, and to the assistant driver's vision to the left.

Elements of the right side of the 155 mm gun barrel, recoil slide, and cradle are seen from the right front. The edges of the armor of the glacis and the drivers' compartment roof overlap the side armor of the sponson. Protruding above the glacis in the foreground is the casting that supported a radio antenna.

Fittings on the glacis and the drivers' compartment roof are observed from the right side. Racks with serrated cutouts for the track pins hold the spare track links in place. A round plug is bolted to the casting for the radio antenna in the foreground. The driver's and assistant driver's cupolas were fixed and did not rotate. The hatch door of each cupola had a mount for a periscope. A combination latch and door handle is visible on each door.

The elements of the gun shown in the preceding photograph are viewed from a closer perspective, permitting a clear view of the right equilibrator. The two equilibrators were pneumatic in operation and served to counterbalance the long gun barrel and lower the amount of manual effort to elevate the gun through the lower angles of elevation. Protruding above the coupling on the rear end of the equilibrator where it is joined to the cradle is the equilibrator-filling valve.

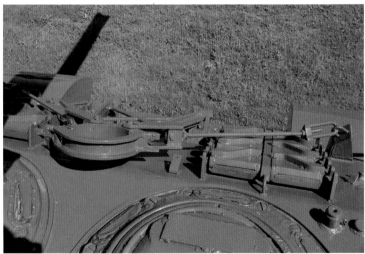

The glacis is viewed from above the assistant driver's cupola, showing the travel lock and its side braces and the spare-track racks. Painted covers have been attached over the openings for the assistant driver's periscopes and vision blocks. To the right front of the assistant driver's cupola is a mount for a spotlight.

The assistant driver's cupola and part of the driver's cupola on an M40 are viewed from above. Casting numbers are visible on the cupola, the hatch door, and the ventilator hood between the two cupolas. The cupola door constituted a frame with hinge fittings; inside the frame was a hood in the form of a flattened dome that rested on a ball-bearing race, allowing the hood and the periscope to be rotated 360 degrees.

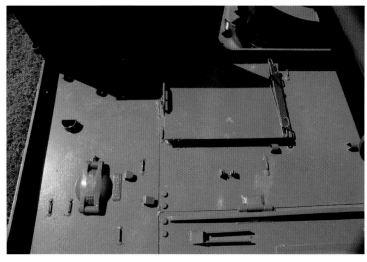

On the left side of the engine deck is an armored cover for a fuel filler. The M40 had four fuel tanks: two vertical thirty-gallon tanks in the front corners of the engine compartment and two fifty-six-gallon horizontal tanks in each sponson, for a total of 172 gallons. The raised plate at the center of the photo is a detachable metal cover over a ventilation grille.

This view of the assistant driver's cupola also includes part of the front end of the engine deck. A ventilation grille is situated below the 155 mm gun barrel, composed of an expanded-mesh grille over shutters. To the right of the grille is a holder for a shovel. To the right of the cupola are two clamps for securing a tow cable. The tube between the hinges of the cupola door contained a spring to assist the occupant in opening and closing the heavy door.

The equilibrators and 155 mm gun barrel to the front of the armored shield are displayed. A U-shaped steel splash guard is welded to the shield around the sighting slot. Affixed to the upper part of each of the trunnion-bearing caps is a rack for storing a projectile loading tray during travel. The racks are mounted on the outer sides of the caps.

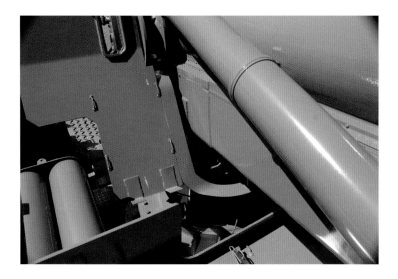

The right side of the armored shield for the 155 mm gun is viewed from the front. The bottom was cut out to provide clearance for the projectile racks seen to the lower left. The shield traversed in unison with the gun. On the shield, the four footman loops and the two angled pieces of metal at the bottom were for securing a folded tarpaulin to the shield.

In a view from the front right corner of the fighting compartment, the right side of the gun shield is to the left, the right projectile racks are toward the right, and the forward armored bulkhead of the fighting compartment is to the front of the racks. A better idea is available here of the size of the two L-shaped tarpaulin holders at the bottom front of the right side of the gun shield.

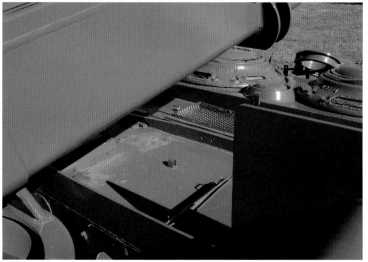

In another view of the front of the right side of the gun shield, more details of the right projectile racks are visible. The projectile tubes were of rolled steel construction, with the seam welded: the weld bead is visible from front to rear on the outboard tube. Also in view are the armored doors on top of the propellant-storage compartments on the right side of the fighting compartment, including the hinges on the outer sides and the combination latch and grab handles on the inboard sides.

In this view from the front right corner of the fighting compartment, the gun cradle is to the upper left, the engine deck is at the center, and the roof of the drivers' compartment is in the foreground. The top of the travel lock is visible to the front of the cupolas. Between the cupolas is a ventilator hood and splash guard.

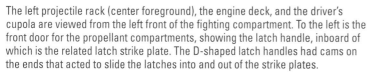

The left projectile rack (center foreground), the engine deck, and the driver's cupola are viewed from the left front of the fighting compartment. To the left is the front door for the propellant compartments, showing the latch handle, inboard of which is the related latch strike plate. The D-shaped latch handles had cams on the ends that acted to slide the latches into and out of the strike plates.

The left side of the gun shield and the left side of the fighting compartment are observed from the front. To the lower left below the front end of the equilibrator is the replenisher cylinder. Like the sighting slot on the right side of the shield, the left sighting slot has a U-shaped splash guard welded around it.

The equilibrators, the upper parts of the trunnion-bearing caps to which the equilibrators are attached, and the upper part of the top carriage of the gun mount are seen from the left front. The elongated retracting eye atop the top carriage of the piece is secured with two large hex screws. The object welded to the gun barrel immediately to the front of the top carriage evidently is a roughly chopped-off chunk of steel to immobilize the gun barrel.

The left projectile racks of an M40 are viewed from the front. The two footman loops on the inboard projectile tube and the two loops on the strip at the top of the forward propellant compartments were for straps for securing a stowed tarpaulin.

Projecting from the left side of the front cap of the gun cradle is the variable-recoil gear cover; extending from the left side of the cover and running along the cradle below the equilibrator is the variable-recoil housing. The variable-recoil mechanism varied the amount of recoil of the gun according to its elevation, with less recoil being allowed at higher elevations. Note the armored filler covers on the engine deck.

As viewed from the left front corner of the fighting compartment, the round object below the gun shield is the traversing gearbox. Below the gearbox, part of the traversing arc is visible; it is attached to the base of the gun mount. To the right is the left projectile rack.

In a view of the center and left side of the engine deck from the front, to the right is an armored cover for a fuel filler, with a raised storage rack to the rear of it. In the shadow at the center of the photo is a similar armored cover for a lubricating-oil filler, to the immediate rear of which is a raised ventilation grille with a metal cover over it.

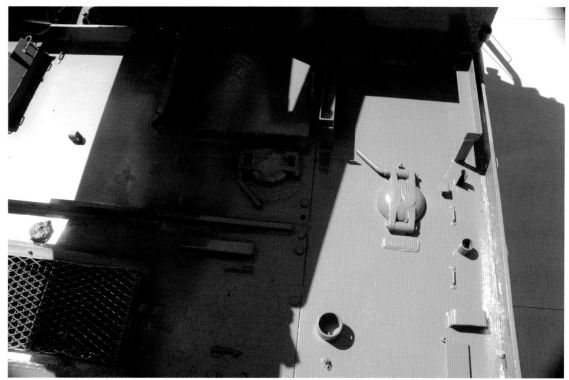

The forward retracting eye of the 155 mm gun is viewed from the left rear. The eye has a flange that is secured to the sleeve of the gun with two large hex screws.

The driver's cupola of this M40 has seen some wear and tear; the rim that holds the rotating center part of the cupola is corroded, and the grab handle is dented. The two small posts with inverted hooks on the tops that are welded on the driver's cupola are attachment points for a removable windshield and driver's hood.

The roof of the driver's compartment, part of the glacis, and part of the engine deck and gun shield are viewed from the left side of the M40. Details of the upper part of the travel lock for the 155 mm gun are evident, primarily the gun saddle yoke, on which the barrel rested during travel, and the top yoke, the curved, clamp-like unit that engaged over the top of the gun barrel.

In the last of the photos of the M40 preserved at Ft. Sill, Oklahoma, the glacis is seen from the left side, focusing on the travel lock and its side braces, the spare track racks, the right brush guard, and the welded-on casting for mounting a radio antenna on the far end of the glacis.

After World War II, the British Army acquired a small number of M40s, designating them 155 mm SP, M40. One such vehicle is preserved at the Imperial War Museum Duxford, at Duxford, England. Note how the top yoke varies in design from the one in the preceding photograph; both of them were valid types as used on M40s. This one was a reversible type that worked with either the 155 mm or 8-inch barrels. *John Blackman*

The IWM Duxford 155 mm SP, M40 skirts around a muddy area at a military vehicle show. The periscopes are installed in the driver's and the assistant driver's cupola hatch doors. A spotlight is mounted to the right front of the assistant driver's cupola. *John Blackman*

The 155 mm SP, M40, at the Imperial War Museum Duxford is viewed from another angle. This vehicle has the mufflers and exhausts mounted on the rear of the engine deck instead of being routed underneath the fighting compartment. A radio antenna is installed in an alternate position to the right rear of the assistant driver's cupola. *John Blackman*

As seen in a photo of the 155 mm SP, M40, at the Imperial War Museum Duxford in storage, most of the components on the front end and midsection of the vehicle appear to be original with a few exceptions, such as the exhaust guards and the spotlight to the right front of the assistant driver's cupola. *Massimo Foti*

The IWM Duxford 155 mm SP, M40, is equipped with T80 tracks, on the running gear and in the racks on the glacis. Three of what appear to be smoke generators are stored with straps on the front of each side of the gun shield. Considerable rust is present on the bare-metal parts of the equilibrators. *Massimo Foti*

This rare 8-inch Howitzer Motor Carriage M43 survives at the US Army Artillery Museum at Ft. Sill, Oklahoma. While some of the more fragile parts are bent or corroded, and the vehicle is in need of fresh paint, the condition is such that complete restoration is possible.

The M43 is viewed from the right rear, showing the spade and the tailgate raised in the travel position. The grated texture of the loading platform, stored on the rear of the tailgate, is apparent. A clear view is available of the exhaust outlet, the box-shaped structure on the lower rear of the hull, above the mount for the tow pintle.

In a left-rear view of the M43, the cable rigging for operating the spade and tailgate is not installed. From most angles, the M43 is easily distinguishable from the M40 by its much shorter artillery piece.

The travel lock is missing from the 155 mm HMC M43 at Ft. Sill, but the mounting brackets for the lock as well as the weldments that served as anchors for the steel-rod braces for the travel lock are present. The service headlights are replacement parts lacking the blackout lamps on top.

The M43 is observed from the rear. The 8-inch howitzer is traversed toward the right. The layout of the framework welded to the underside of the tailgate is partially visible. Also in view are the three hinges at the bottom of the tailgate.

The small platform on the right rear of the M43 is illustrated. Jutting from the rear of the hull above the platform is an external power receptacle and cover, above which is the right locking link for the spade, secured to the related bracket on the hull. On the diagonal support for the platform is welded a hand rail.

Further details of the spade assembly are illustrated. The arms of the spade are composed of I-beam- and T-beam-type steel structures, welded together. The X-shaped brace between the legs of the spade were fabricated from steel T-beams.

The raised spade of the M43 is viewed from the right side. Each of the steel teeth on the lower edge of the spade was attached to the spade with two hex screws, set into round recesses in the tooth, and secured with hex nuts on the other side of the spade surface.

Below the hinge for the spade arm, a steel bumper with a cupped design is welded to the hull; there is a similar one below the left spade arm, and these were designed to act as stops for the spade when it was being dug into the ground prior to firing.

At the center of the rear of the hull below the tailgate is the exhaust outlet, a welded-steel assembly with an opening at the top. The lower part of the rear of the outlet is curved. Near the top is a rectangular tab that protrudes to the rear, below which is a slot through the steel, not visible from this angle but evident in other photographs. Below the exhaust outlet is a mount for a tow pintle.

In a view of the rear of the hull toward the left, the design of the left support arm for the tailgate is evident. This is the unit to the front of the left side of the cross-brace of the spade with the flared bottom. To the left of the bottom of that support arm is the left spade hinge, below which is the idler.

Structural details of the underside, or rear, of the tailgate are revealed in this photo from the left rear of the M43 at Ft. Sill. The left support arm, pointed out in the preceding photo, is the tapering structure under the tailgate. Also in view is the left locking link for the tailgate and spade.

This view of the left side of the fighting compartment of the M43 shows the traversing hand wheel, the storage box for the panoramic telescope, the elevating sector, and the left side of the howitzer carriage. Partially visible in the front corner of the compartment is the base of the universal projectile rack, which held eight shells. A similar rack is on the right side of the compartment.

Around the base of the howitzer mount in the M43 are hinged, diamond-tread floor plates with folding grab handles. Note the triangular lightening hole in the support for the elevating hand wheel and shaft.

The universal projectile rack in the front left of the fighting compartment is viewed from a different angle. It was designed to hold either 8-inch or 155 mm shells and thus was interchangeable between the M43 and the M40. At the bottom is the left travel lock for the howitzer cradle. There was one on each side, secured to the floor with a large eye or staple and secured at the other end to a hook on each side of the cradle.

Although the breech block, the counterbalance to the upper right of the breech ring, and other components are missing, this view gives an idea of most of the main elements of the right side of the breech, the cradle, and the carriage of an 8-inch howitzer. To the left, touching the rear of the breech ring, is the tailgate.

The elevating hand wheel and gearbox of the 8-inch howitzer is shown. Missing below the hand wheel is the elevating hand wheel brake and stirrup, which it was necessary to depress before operating the hand wheel. To the right is the right universal projectile rack.

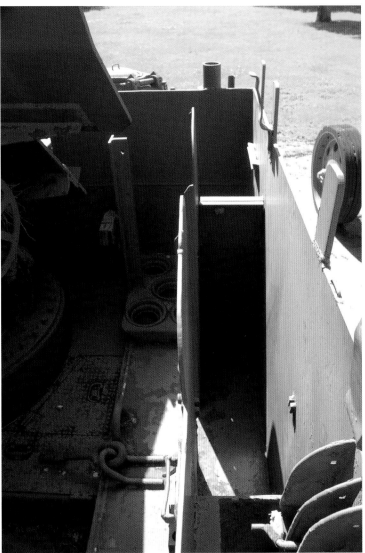

In a view of the right side of the fighting compartment of the M43, in the background is the right projectile rack, and along the right side are storage compartments for bagged powder charges.

The M43's 8-inch howitzer is viewed from below along the right side of the vehicle. Jutting from the left side of the front cap of the howitzer cradle is the variable-recoil gear cover, which protected a mechanism that reduced the amount of the howitzer's recoil when elevated at high angles.

In this photograph of the left equilibrator and the 8-inch howitzer barrel and cradle, the equipment on the side of the cradle below the front end of the equilibrator are the variable recoil housing (upper) and the replenisher assembly (below).

The assistant driver's cupola is in the foreground in this view of the 8-inch howitzer and the armor at the front of the fighting compartment. A holder for a five-gallon liquid container has been welded to the engine deck inboard of the vertical pipe on the front of the fighting compartment. The purpose of that pipe and its companion on the opposite side is unclear.

The thickness of the frontal bulkhead armor of the fighting compartment of the M43 is apparent in this photograph. To the front of the bulkhead, covers have been placed over the ventilation grilles on the rear of the engine deck.

The 8-inch M43 Howitzer Motor Carriage, shown here during training, was the stable mate to the M40 Gun Motor Carriage. Produced in modest numbers, the type saw combat in Korea, where it performed admirably. *National Archives and Records Administration*